A Bison's Tale

THIS EDITION

Editorial Management by Oriel Square
Produced for DK by WonderLab Group LLC
Jennifer Emmett, Erica Green, Kate Hale, *Founders*

Editor Maya Myers; **Photography Editor** Nicole DiMella; **Managing Editor** Rachel Houghton;
Designers Project Design Company; **Researcher** Michelle Harris;
Copy Editor Lori Merritt; **Indexer** Connie Binder; **Proofreader** Susan K. Hom;
Sensitivity Reader Dr. Naomi R. Caldwell; **Series Reading Specialist** Dr. Jennifer Albro

First American Edition, 2024
Published in the United States by DK Publishing, a division of Penguin Random House LLC
1745 Broadway, 20th Floor, New York, NY 10019

Copyright © 2024 Dorling Kindersley Limited
24 25 26 27 10 9 8 7 6 5 4 3 2 1
001–339781–Jun/2024

All rights reserved.
Without limiting the rights under the copyright reserved above, no part of this publication may be reproduced, stored in or introduced into a retrieval system, or transmitted, in any form, or by any means (electronic, mechanical, photocopying, recording, or otherwise), without the prior written permission of the copyright owner.
Published in Great Britain by Dorling Kindersley Limited

A catalog record for this book is available from the Library of Congress.
HC ISBN: 978-0-7440-9438-1
PB ISBN: 978-0-7440-9437-4

DK books are available at special discounts when purchased in bulk for sales promotions, premiums, fund-raising, or educational use. For details, contact:
DK Publishing Special Markets, 1745 Broadway, 20th Floor, New York, NY 10019
SpecialSales@dk.com

Printed and bound in China

The publisher would like to thank the following for their kind permission to reproduce their images: a=above; c=center; b=below; l=left; r=right; t=top; b/g=background
vendor: Alamy Stock Photo: Associated Press / Douglas C. Pizac 17br, Peter Elvin 11bc, Gon2Foto / Richard Mittleman 23bl, North Wind Picture Archives / Nancy Carter 17bl; **Dreamstime.com:** Andreanita 18bc, Artur Balitskii 16bc, Sean Beckett 19cb, John Blumenkamp 9bc, Donyanedomam 1, 14–15, Andreas Edelmann 9bc, Veniamin Kraskov 6bc, Geoffrey Kuchera 3, Aleksas Kvedoras 20bc, Manuellacoste 6–7, Outdoorsman 12–13, Pancaketom 14bc, Denis Pepin 15bc, Jerry S 23cl, Andrew Sentipal 12bc, Samuel Strickler 13bl, Kelly Vandellen 21bl, Tracey Vivar 10–11, Nico De Wal 13bc, Zayacskz 20–21; **First Nations Development Institute:** 7br; **Getty Images:** Cavan Images 4–5, Westend61 23clb; **Getty Images / iStock:** Betty4240 22, KenCanning 18–19, Pimpay 8bc, Oleg Sibiriakov 10bc, Vital_Gertsik 4l, 8bc (background), 10bc (background), 16bc (background); **Native Stock Pictures:** 16–17; **naturepl.com:** Ingo Arndt 11bl; **Shutterstock.com:** Grey Mountain Photo 8–9, Don Mammoser 21br, Melissa Schalke 23cla; **U.S. National Park Service:** Jacob W. Frank 15bl, 23tl

Cover images: *Front:* **Dreamstime.com:** Martin Fredskov clb, Ievgen Melamud cb; Getty Images / iStock: Digitalvision Vectors / Diane555 (Background); *Back:* **Shutterstock.com:** Pogorelova Olga cra

All other images © Dorling Kindersley Limited
For more information see: www.dkimages.com

www.dk.com

This book was made with Forest Stewardship Council™ certified paper – one small step in DK's commitment to a sustainable future.
Learn more at
www.dk.com/uk/information/sustainability

Pre-level

A Bison's Tale

Angela Modany

It is summer in the grassland.
This is the bison's home.
The bison is a big mammal.

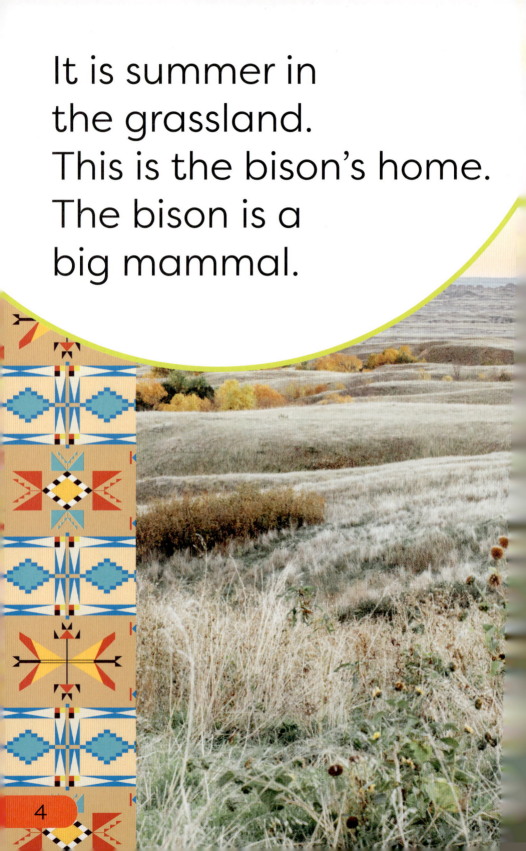

The bison is the biggest land animal in North America.

The bison eats grass. It eats grass almost all day. Grass gives the bison energy.

grass

People know the bison needs grass. People protect the grassland.

The bison is strong.
It has two sharp horns.
Two bison hit horns to
show they are strong.

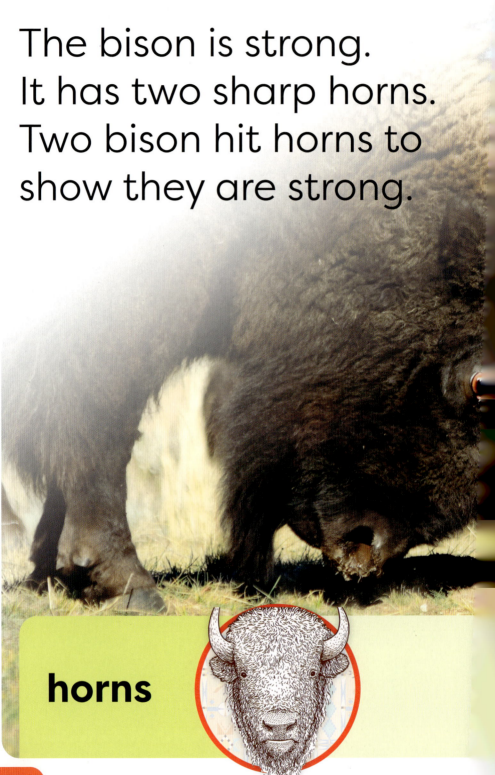

horns

People watch the bison's tail. The tail stands up when the bison is on guard. The people stay far away. They respect the bison. They give it space.

tail

A group of bison is called a herd.
A herd of bison moves across the grassland.
The bison walk in a line.

herd

They come to a river.
They cross the river.
The bison are
good swimmers.

The weather is cool. The bison gets ready for winter.

fur

It grows thicker fur. The fur will keep the bison warm.

People get ready for winter.
The bison can give them food and shelter.

shelter

The bison can help the people survive.
The people thank the bison.
They sing songs about the bison.

Winter comes.
Fur keeps the
bison warm.
The bison moves snow
with its head.
There is grass
for the bison
to eat.

snow

The snow melts
in spring.
The bison sheds
its winter fur.
It rolls on the ground.
It makes a ditch.
Some fur falls off
in the ditch.

spring

A bison calf is born.
The calf follows
its mother.
The mother feeds
her calf milk.
The calf grows.
The herd grows bigger.

Glossary

calf
a baby bison

energy
a body's ability to move

grassland
land with many grasses instead of trees

shed
to lose from an animal's body

strong
having great power

Quiz

Answer the questions to see what you have learned. Check your answers with an adult.

1. Where do bison live?
2. What do bison eat?
3. How do people know to stay away from a bison?
4. How do bison stay warm in the winter?
5. What is a baby bison called?

1. Grassland 2. Grass 3. They watch its tail 4. They grow thick fur 5. A calf